'We couldn't afford to keep the family car'

THE BEST OF

2008

D1344959

MATTHEW PRITCHETT

studied at St Martin's School of Art in London and first saw himself published in the *New Statesman* during one of its rare lapses from high seriousness. He has been the *Daily Telegraph*'s front-page pocket cartoonist since 1988. In 1995, 1996, 1999, 2005 and 2006 he was the winner of the Cartoon Arts Trust Award and in 1991, 2004 and 2006 he was 'What the Papers Say' Cartoonist of the Year. In 1996, 1998, 2000 and 2008 he was *UK Press Gazette* Cartoonist of the Year and in 2002 he received an MBE.

Own your favourite Matt cartoons. Browse a range of Matt cartoons from 2003 onwards and buy online at **www.telegraph.co.uk/photographs** or call 020 7931 2076.

The Daily Telegraph

THE BEST OF

MATT

2008

An Orion paperback

First published in Great Britain in 2008 by
Orion Books
A division of the Orion Publishing Group Ltd
Orion House
5 Upper St Martin's Lane
London WC2H 9EA
An Hachette Livre UK company

10 9 8 7 6 5 4 3 2 1

A CIP catalogue record for this book
is available from the British Library

ISBN 978 0 7528 9364 8

Printed in the UK by CPI William Clowes
Beccles NR34 7TL

The Orion Publishing Group's policy is to use papers that
are natural, renewable and recyclable products and
made from wood grown in sustainable forests. The logging
and manufacturing processes are expected to conform to
the environmental regulations of the country of origin.

www.orionbooks.co.uk

'If it's in the catchment area
of a good school and an
NHS dentist, we'll take it'

THE BEST OF
MATT
2008

IN PRAISE OF MATT

by Sir Terry Wogan

I realise that I'm leaning against an open door when extolling the virtues of Matt. Even his fellow national newspaper cartoonists acknowledge his supremacy; his brilliant work is the yardstick by which the rest are judged. Any humorist will tell you how hard it is to be funny to order, even once a week. This man does it every day, week and year, and illustrates it into the bargain. . .

Those wonderful, deceptively simple, spare drawings, so easy that, rather like Bing Crosby's crooning, you think 'I can do that!' Don't even bother trying. Art concealing art is a well-worn cliché, but it sums up Matt's pocket cartoons. In just a couple of strokes we get the picture and there, in the forefront, are the familiar, unmistakeable Matt characters: two little dots for eyes, matchstick legs, same nose and mouth. One with mouth wide open as if shouting, the other non-plussed, lugubrious. They make you smile even before you get to the punch-line but, search as you may, you'll never find them smiling. I know – I've had every Yearbook since he started. Matt's men and women are serious, morose, glum. They take life seriously, misanthropically, as do his dogs, cats, chickens, polar bears and other animals. Even his inanimate objects give off an air of gloom and despondency. That's what makes these little slices of life so funny; that, and the words underneath, those matchless, topical, relevant, right-on-the-money words.

How does he do it? Every day a witty, sharp gem of social comment that's as up-to-date as the headlines and always, as the UK Press Awards once said, consistently funny. Anybody 'round here ever see a duff Matt cartoon? I suppose, for the purposes of this paean of praise, I should have asked the man himself to give us some kind of indication of how he does it, but I know him well enough to know that he'd look at me in that kindly, gentle way of his, shrug his shoulders, and change the subject. The truth is, he doesn't know how he does it; he just turns up every morning at the *Telegraph* and does. Easy, when you're a genius . . .

THE BEST OF

The Last
20 Years

'Can I come out in Sympathy?'

'You were bound to be recaptured, hanging around a departure lounge for 20 hours'

1988

Prison officers and air traffic controllers strike

'I'm knitting a "NO STRIKE AGREEMENT" notice for the midwives'

'I'd like to change my name to D658WCN'

DVLA to sell personalised number plates

'I think we can afford the first incision, nurse'

'Don't heat it right through. I don't want them thinking we can't afford a microwave'

Health fears

Train strikes

'Oh dear, I've started picking up satellite TV'

'I don't think this counts as
swimming the Channel, sir'

'There's a 10p fine every
time you say "It's the end
of an era"'

Thatcher resigns

'I doubt if we'll see
European monetary union
in our lifetime'

'He's captured brilliantly
the lack of facilities,
transport and cheap
housing in rural areas'

'This train has always been
called the 8.57, but nobody
can remember why'

'The vicar's trying to
compete with the Sunday-
opening supermarkets'

Painting stolen

'We're the three wise men'

'On second thoughts, could I
have my brick back?'

'It's a marvel of evolution –
an out-of-worker bee'

'Just get up there, stand
on the edge and think of
the economy'

'A lot of the pageantry has
gone since the defence cuts'

1993

'Police? Can you see with your High Street video camera if the greengrocer has any broccoli?'

Pound plummets

'If I hadn't got out a copy of the Maastricht treaty they would never have left'

1994

'Passengers waiting for the 13.22 are advised to use a high factor sun cream'

Rail strikes

Cushy prisons

Germans ban beef on D-Day

'At least we know you're not taking performance-enhancing drugs'

'He's not stuck, he's protesting against the M65'

'I bought these on Saturday
but I now realise I was coming
out of recession too fast'

'Can a bishop go
either way?'

C of E condones gay bishop

1996

'Scratch away the surface
to reveal three Cezannes
and win £50,000'

Protesters try to stop
Newbury bypass

Mad Cow Disease

1997

'Scientists have discovered a link between not eating your greens and being hit with a saucepan'

'Daddy, why does Tony Blair allow earthquakes to happen?'

'And Damien Hirst did the tail fin on this one'

BA replace union flag with tailfin artworks

'If you don't want to know
how your marriage ends,
look away now'

'I'm worried it
might crash when we
go from BC to AD'

Concerns begin early for
the new millennium

President Clinton has
girl(s) trouble

'Or, if you want something more expensive, I can show you this again tomorrow'

'Isn't it time you were abolished, dear?'

Lords reform

'Same again?'

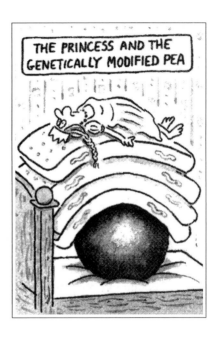

2000

Fishing in crisis . . .

and Rover in crisis

'WAIT! . . . I can make RoboDog wave goodbye'

'. . . and I got that one for my bombing raids on Kosovo'

Inaccurate bombing

'Let them eat cake'

2002

'Day return?
Feeling lucky, sir?'

'Hello, have any of your
CCTV cameras spotted a
policeman anywhere?'

'I wish I had gay parents'

Anti-prejudice laws

'I'd love to come for a pint, I'll just check with the "pocket of resistance"'

Troops in Iraq

'We're remaking "Brief Encounter" – there are no trains and it ends with a gay wedding'

'To be honest, I just follow
the rest of the market'

2004

'This is so much better than sniffing each other's bottoms'

'The 45 minute claim didn't refer to the pizza'

WMD threat

'I'm just ringing to say my
test is going brilliantly'

'I'm on the Atkins diet –
I don't know if I'm
allowed coconuts'

2005

'We're going to have
to shoot the staff'

'It's half-past two, fatty'

Hunting ban

'The phoney apathy is over –
it's time for the real thing'

Election date announced

'If I had to choose, I'd rather John Prescott punched me...'

'What do we want?
Why did we come here?
What were we saying?'

'That's the most impressive case of bird flu I've ever seen'

2007

'*Apparently, by 2010 you'll be obese and I'll be Polish*'

'*Well, the Britishness classes seem to be working*'

'Do you want to cling on for coffee or leave while you're still popular?'

'It's stopped spinning and now it's going on a lecture tour of the US'

Blair to go . . .

'Look what someone gave me
in exchange for our house'

THE BEST OF
2008

'Dour is the new cool'

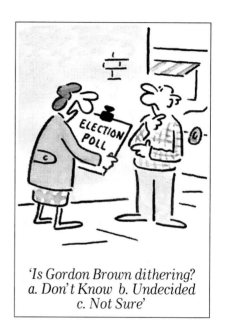

'Is Gordon Brown dithering?
a. Don't Know b. Undecided
c. Not Sure'

Gordon takes over

Gordon's honeymoon causes problems for Tories

'My father's at that age
where I wish I could find a
nice, small political party
for him to lead'

Media focus on Menzies
Campbell's age . . .

'I'd like to have him neutered
– he's the Nick Clegg of
the neighbourhood'

. . . and Nick Clegg's lovers

Government loses personal data

Labour's donations scrutinised

'My dad is an MP and the
tooth fairy left me £45,000'

'Good work, Teddy, I'm
giving you a £30,000 bonus'

MPs pay family members

Politics

'Listen, men. Stealing from the poor hasn't been as popular as I'd hoped...'

'I'm canvassing on behalf of the Labour party'

10p tax u-turn

'We'd have won Crewe if it wasn't for a few disgruntled car drivers . . . and home owners . . . and people who buy food'

'I suggest we stop listening and we start putting our fingers in our ears and shouting la-la-la'

'We don't know how to remove
a prime minister – Gordon
always took care of all that'

'At any moment I'm only
45 minutes away from buying
Alastair Campbell's book'

Political memoirs

'I saw that incompetent
Minister in the street…no, the
other one…not her…no, not
him…you know…'

'If MPs' pay goes up too much
there's a danger Tony Blair
will come back'

Credit Crunch

'For goodness sake, man!
House prices aren't a suitable
topic for dinner parties'

'How much is this house?
.........And how much is
it now?'

'As you can see, this property has spectacular views of the recession'

'Fortunately the food price inflation cancels out the fall in house prices'

Credit Crunch

'I tried to buy a cheese roll for lunch but I was gazumped'

'Give me back that bread!'

'I always knew our life of
hedonistic excess would
have to come to an end'

'Let me get straight to the
point – do you have
any gold fillings?'

Credit Crunch

'The trampolines help them
to follow the markets'

'I got out of cash and
into plastic carrier bags'

'I splashed out and spent all
our disposable income on
two plastic carrier bags'

The 5p carrier bag

Run on the Bank

'Leave your money where it is'

'You want to borrow
a pen? No'

'I never know the difference;
is this a simile or
a metaphor?'

'We're worried about your finances and we'd like to withdraw our pocket money'

'I've decided to withdraw our savings'

'Why don't you consolidate
all your reckless loans into
one giant mistake?'

'Your savings have become
exposed to American
sub-prime mortgages'

Run on the Bank

'They didn't have any money'

'Do you have any old clothes you can spare? I'm donating a bag of stuff to the bank'

'For a laugh, a bunch of us are
going to form a queue outside
another high street bank'

'I started a false rumour
about this motorway so
we'd have a clear run'

Rumours abound . . .

'There's that nice couple we met in the queue outside Northern Rock'

Panic switches to fuel

'Never mind the car,
is the petrol all right?'

'Sorry, we can't afford
to run a car'

'When I mention road taxes I want you to perform an emergency stop, get out of the car and catch a bus'

'Will you sponsor me to drive my family car ten miles?'

'If I had 5p I'd buy a plastic bag to put over my head'

'I stole your car a month ago and it's nearly bankrupted me'

'I admit it, there is someone else. I've been seeing the postman – but not very often'

'A less frequent service? You've been talking to the bin men, haven't you?'

'We take our rubbish on
holiday and hope that the
airline loses it'

'Next day guarantee? That's
the letter, not the post office'

'Come in, Mum. You'll never guess what this used to be'

'42 days? I didn't know I was putting recyclable waste into the wrong wheelie bin...'

Binge Britain

'I never have more
than one glass'

'This won't help to curb
middle-class drinking'

Rugby World Cup

'Are you sure this
is your homework?'

'The can of cider makes
you look ten years younger'

Binge Britain

'You have three children. How lovely. And what are they – obese or drunk?'

'A levels may be easier, but you're forgetting that most teenagers are drunk when they take them'

'You don't stink of cigarettes.
Have you been in
the pub again?'

'We are time travellers from
the year 2050'

'Red meat, chips and wine?
Do you mind paying the
bill before you eat?'

'Sorry, I now have to wear
this every time I sell a
packet of cigarettes'

Health

'Don't eat that rubbish –
they're full of additives'

'Let's be frank: if we're going
back to your place, should I
buy some fruit and veg?'

'My wife gave me this jumper and I gave her the vomiting bug'

'There's something nasty
going round at the
moment... it's called the
Health Secretary'

'Why don't you work in
a job centre? You might meet
a nice young doctor'

NHS troubles

NHS troubles

'I didn't realise there'd be
so much paperwork'

'How disappointing; I hoped
we wouldn't see you
back inside'

Police protest and prison officers strike

'I believe you reported
some intruders'

'POLICE! STOP! I've got
you surrounded'

Home owners' rights

Sharia Law

'Wow, some of these C of E fanatics are terrifying'

'Since the pub and post office shut, the surveillance camera is the hub of village life'

'Sorry I'm late. The train was delayed, I was stopped by security and then held for 42 days'

'We always go private for
our terrorism'

'A concrete barrier a day
keeps the doctor away'

Medical students accused of terror attack

BBC standards questioned

BBC standards questioned

The Jet Set

'Apparently they can hold us here for 42 days'

'There's no information, the food is terrible and they've lost my banner'

'Would you also photograph
my suitcase, so I have
something to remember it by?'

'Not security, we're seeing
if you have any more
money we could take'

'I've heard Royalty is in the area'

Harry in Afghanistan

'I was flying over the Sandringham Estate when somebody shot me'

Protected birds shot

THOSE ROYAL BLACKMAIL PICTURES

'I told everyone we were
at Wimbledon'

'It's not wetter. It's just
that your fear of getting wet
has increased'

'You've built your new houses
on a flood plain'

Weather

'We're solved the problem
of rowdy drunks in
the town centre'

'You're the first sandbag in
our family ever to go
to Oxford'

'I phoned our neighbours to remind them to water our garden and they were a little bit short with me'

'It's getting chilly – throw the Al Gore DVD on the fire'

'I shouldn't be stuck in the
office on a day like this;
I should be in a traffic jam'

Roses are red,
Daffodils are flutey,
My love for you grows
In line with fuel duty

Roses are red,
But take some affording,
I confess that I love you
– Without water-boarding

Obama Fever

The race begins

'I ate your mince pie. You were in the kitchen for so long I presumed you were dead'

'Don't forget my mother is staying for Christmas'

And finally...

Missing man reappears

And finally...

'Left at Tesco, go past two
Tescos, right at the next Tesco
and it's opposite Tesco'

'How long has that
been there?'

'There will be nobody
left in Poland'

And finally...

'This is my husband; I call
him the "Ordinary One"'

'Seven and a quarter inches
of beer, please'

'Listen, whatever your name is, think of the tax benefits for married couples'

'Let's broaden our horizons, let's be miserable in another country'

And finally...

'He brought opera to the masses – I'll never forgive him for that'

'Hello...oh sorry, I can't
talk...I'm driving'

Mobile phone law

'There's been an explosion
at the wind farm'

And finally...

'...and when Jeremy Beadle opens the gate...'

'Just because you have to do what you're told doesn't mean you're being indoctrinated by terrorists'

'A pilot misses the runway by 200 yards and is called a hero, I miss the garage by a few feet...'

'And they wonder why we drink'

And finally...

'I'm pleased to see how few people have travelled here today'

'Maybe it's because I'm Etonian, that I love London so...'

Boris becomes Mayor

'...but am I happy and
fulfilled enough to be
cooked by Jamie Oliver?'

'My accountant just told
me to drop dead'

And finally...

'I'm sorry, but your numbers
have to be controlled'

'Did you know that your
kidneys are on eBay?'

And finally...

'I'm writing a list of people
I want to see detained
without charge'

42 days detention

'It's terrible, I'm spending
nearly £1 a week on food'

'I'm not buying a magazine;
I'll read one of the Top Secret
documents left on the train'

'It's very sad, but nobody
knows what makes an
MP suddenly resign'

David Davis resigns

And finally...

'This is the police. We've got you partially surrounded'

'I just want to be fit enough
to go and see my GP'

'Maybe acupuncture doesn't
work for dandruff'

And finally…

'It can't be wrong, it's guided by satellites'

GARDEN CENTRE

TERRACOTTA!

YOU'VE SEEN THE ARMY, NOW BUY THE FLOWER POTS